Very useful machines
# Levers

Chris Oxlade

# www.heinemann.co.uk/library
Visit our website to find out more information about Heinemann Library books.

To order:
☎ Phone 44 (0) 1865 888066
📄 Send a fax to 44 (0) 1865 314091
💻 Visit the Heinemann Bookshop at www.heinemann.co.uk/library to browse our catalogue and order online.

First published in Great Britain by Heinemann Library, Halley Court, Jordan Hill, Oxford OX2 8EJ, part of Harcourt Education.
Heinemann is a registered trademark of Harcourt Education Ltd.

© Harcourt Education Ltd 2003
First published in paperback in 2004
The moral right of the proprietor has been asserted.

Editorial: Nicole Irving and Georga Godwin
Design: Jo Hinton-Malivoire, Richard Parker and AMR
Picture Research: Rebecca Sodergren and Pete Morris
Production: Séverine Ribierre

Originated by Ambassador Litho Ltd
Printed and bound in China by South China Printing Company

ISBN 0 431 17892 5 (hardback)
07 06 05 04 03
10 9 8 7 6 5 4 3 2 1

ISBN 0 431 17898 4 (paperback)
08 07 06 05 04
10 9 8 7 6 5 4 3 2 1

## British Library Cataloguing in Publication Data
Oxlade, Chris
Levers – Very Useful Machines
621.8'11
A full catalogue record for this book is available from the British Library.

## Acknowledgements
The Publishers would like to thank the following for permission to reproduce photographs: Alamy Images **pp. 8**, **15**, **25**; Anthony Blake Ohoto Library **p. 14**; Construction Photography **pp. 24**, **29**; Corbis/Barry Lewis **p. 5**; Corbis/Onne Van Der Wal **p. 27**; Corbis/Robert Maass **p. 23**; Corbis/Royalty-Free **p. 18**; Garden Picture Library/Lamontagne **p. 6**; Pete Morris **pp. 4**, **9**, **10**, **11**, **12**, **17**, **19**, **20**, **22**, **26**; Trevor Clifford **pp. 7**, **13**, **16**; TRIP/H Rogers **p. 21**.

Cover photograph of a man unscrewing a nut reproduced with permission of Corbis/ Lester Lefkowitz.

Every effort has been made to contact copyright holders of any material reproduced in this book. Any omissions will be rectified in subsequent printings if notice is given to the Publishers.

# Contents

Any words appearing in the text in bold, **like this**, are explained in the Glossary.

# What is a lever?

lever

A machine is a man-made **device**. All machines make our lives easier by helping us to do jobs. This simple machine is called a lever.

A lever is a very useful machine.
These people are using levers to lift a
heavy log. Without the levers, it would
be impossible to move the log.

# What does a lever do?

A lever makes a pull or a push. This garden fork is a lever. Pulling back on the fork handle will push the soil forwards.

pulling back on handle

pushing forwards on soil

Pushes and pulls from levers can also squash, grip and cut things. The handles of this nut cracker are levers. Pressing them together breaks open the nut.

# Parts of a lever

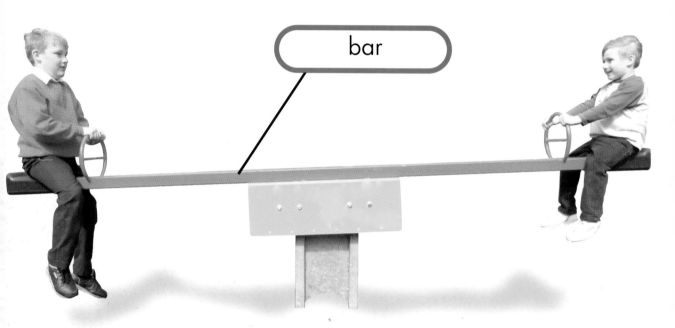

bar

A lever is a very simple machine. To make a lever you just need a strong **rod** or a bar. A see-saw is a lever. It is made with a strong wooden or metal bar.

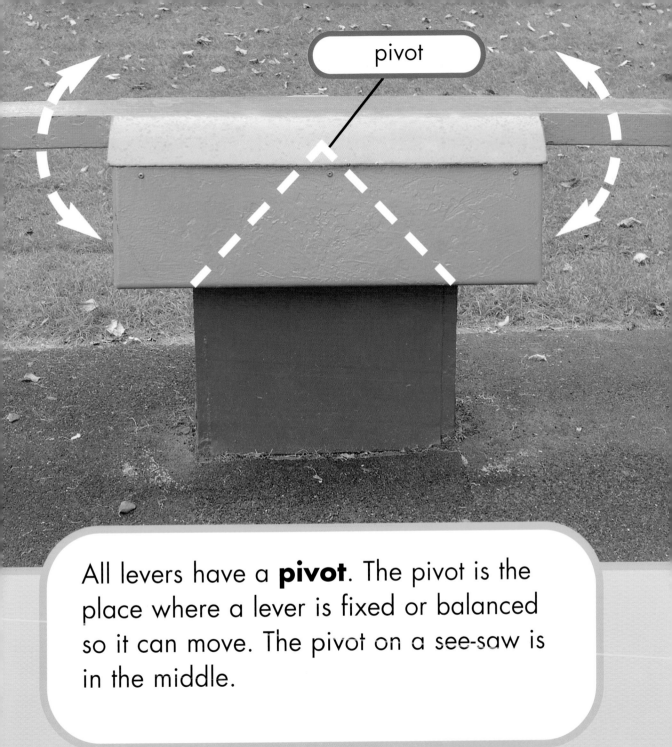

pivot

All levers have a **pivot**. The pivot is the place where a lever is fixed or balanced so it can move. The pivot on a see-saw is in the middle.

# How does a lever work?

load

We often use levers to lift things. The weight of the thing pushes down on the lever. This push is called a **load**. Here, the load is the weight of the drain cover.

effort

A person pushes or pulls on a lever to make it turn. This push or pull is called an **effort**. Here, the person pushes down on the bar with an effort. This will lift up the drain cover.

# Levers together

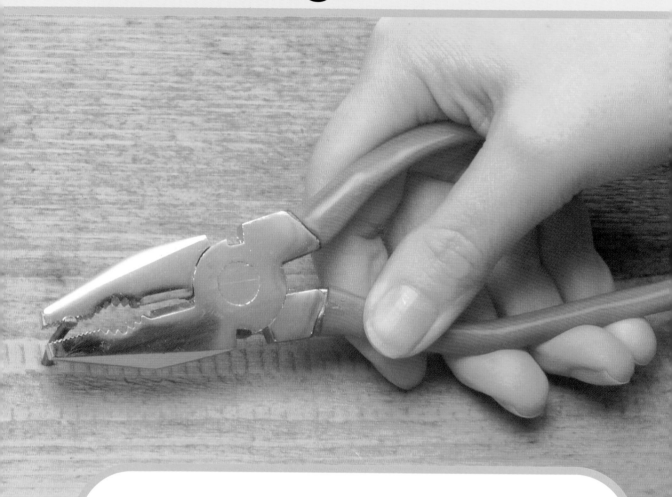

Here are two simple devices, each with two levers joined in the middle with a **pivot**. Pushing the handles of these pliers pushes the jaws together to grip the nail.

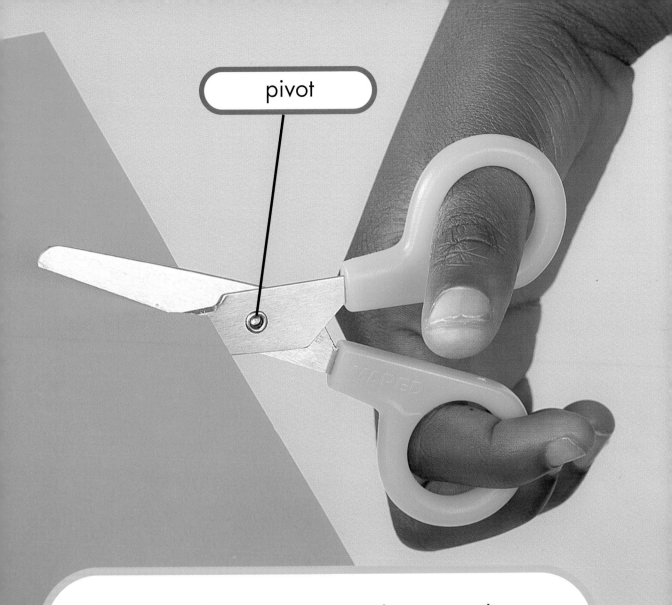

pivot

This pair of scissors is two levers with a pivot in the middle. Pushing the handles together pushes the blades together. The blades then cut the paper.

13

# Pivots at the end

These levers have a **pivot** at the end. This garlic press has two levers joined by a pivot. Because the garlic is near the pivot, the push on it is very strong.

A wheelbarrow is also a lever. The wheel is the pivot. The salt in this barrow is the **load**. Pulling up on the handles with an **effort** lifts the load so it can be moved.

# More levers

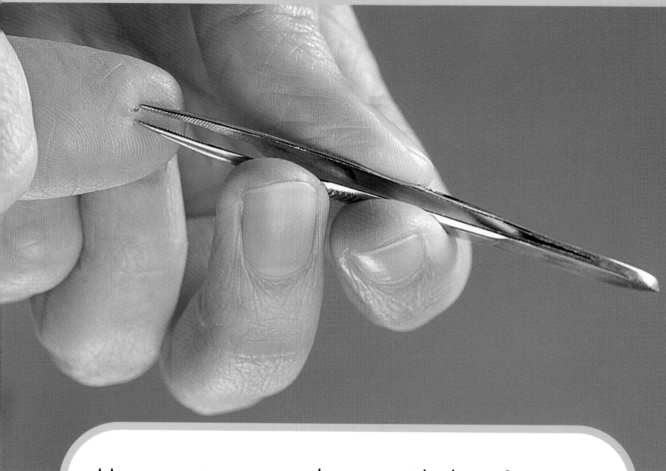

Here are two more levers with the **pivot** at the end. This time, though, you push or pull nearer the pivot. Tweezers make your **effort** smaller so you do not crush **delicate** things.

The top of this stapler is a lever. Its pivot is attached to the stapler's base. When you press hard on the stapler, it pushes a staple through the paper.

# Levers for cutting

This is a paper cutter. The handle and blade are a long lever. The lever makes it easy to cut lots of sheets of paper at the same time.

Garden shears have two levers joined by a **pivot**. Pushing the handles together on these shears moves the blades over each other to slice through the branch.

# Levers for turning

Levers help us to turn things as well. A spanner is a lever. You use it to tighten or loosen a **nut** or **bolt**. Pulling or pushing on the spanner's handle makes the nut or bolt turn round.

Using a long lever makes it easier to turn a nut or bolt. This is a wheel brace for tightening or loosening the nuts on a wheel. It has a long handle.

# Working levers

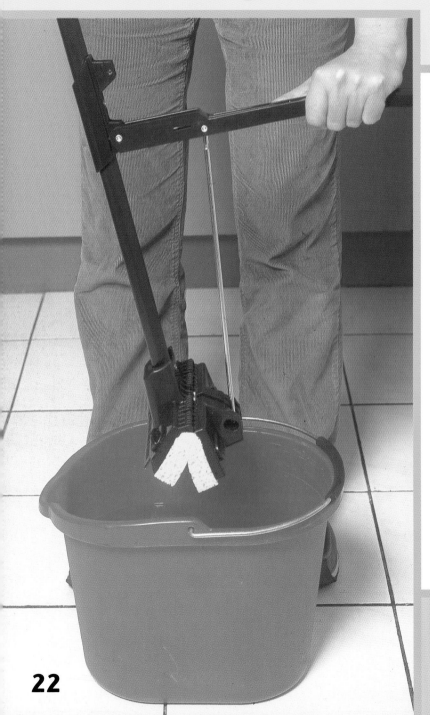

Some levers are used to work other machines. This floor mop has a lever on its handle. Pushing down on the lever squeezes the sponge tightly to wring out dirty water.

This machine is a water pump. It pumps water for drinking and cooking from deep underground. The long handle is a lever that makes it easier to work the pump.

# Levers for digging

**Mechanical** diggers use lots of levers. The lever on the end of the digger's arm moves and lifts the heavy bucket full of earth and rocks.

ram

The levers on the digger's arm need very strong pushes and pulls to make them move. Powerful **rams**, like mechanical **muscles**, do the pushing and pulling.

# Levers in control

Levers are useful to control complicated machines. A bicycle has levers that make the brakes work. When you pull the brake handles, rubber blocks press hard against the wheels, slowing the bike down.

A sailor steers a **dinghy** with a **tiller**. The tiller is a lever. Pushing and pulling on the tiller moves a flat piece of wood called the rudder. This makes the boat turn.

# Amazing lever facts

- The lower part of your arm works just like a lever. Your elbow is the **pivot** and your **muscles** move it.
- The lever is one of the oldest machines in the world. It was invented thousands of years ago.
- The long ladder on top of a fire engine is a lever. Its pivot is on the fire engine.
- There are more than 250 levers in a piano.
- In each of your ears there are three tiny bones that work like little levers.

- A lifting bridge is made of two huge levers that lift up to let ships pass underneath. Bridges like this are called bascule bridges.

# Glossary

**bolt**    metal rod with a screw thread on the outside

**delicate**    can be damaged easily

**device**    thing that does a job. A clothes peg is a device. So is an electronic calculator.

**dinghy**    small sailing boat for one or two people

**effort**    push or pull on a lever that you use to make the lever move

**load**    push or pull on a lever from the thing the lever is trying to lift or move or squash

**mechanical**    something usually worked by machinery

**muscle**    part of the body used for movement, such as walking or lifting

| | |
|---|---|
| **nut** | piece of metal or plastic with four or six sides and a hole in the centre. There is a screw thread inside the hole so that the nut can be screwed on to a bolt. |
| **pivot** | place on a lever where the lever is fixed so that it can turn round |
| **ram** | machine that looks like a bicycle pump and makes a huge push or pull |
| **rod** | long, thin, strong piece of material |
| **tiller** | bar that a sailor pushes and pulls to steer a small boat |

# More books to read

*Levers*, Angela Royston (Heinemann Library, 2000)
*What do Levers do?*, David Glover (Heinemann Library, 1996)
*Levers*, Michael Dahl (Franklin Watts, 2001)
*Toybox Science: Levers*, Chris Ollerenshaw and Pat Triggs (A and C Black, 2001)

# Index